Rock Guitar Licks

Interior design and layout: Len Vogler

This book Copyright © 2000 by Amsco Publications,
A Division of Music Sales Corporation, New York

Order No. AM 962412
US International Standard Book Number: 0.8256.1785.5
UK International Standard Book Number: 0.7119.8020.9

Exclusive Distributors:
Music Sales Corporation
257 Park Avenue South, New York, NY 10010 USA
Music Sales Limited
8/9 Frith Street, London W1V 5TZ England
Music Sales Pty. Limited
120 Rothschild Street, Rosebery, Sydney, NSW 2018, Australia

Printed in the United States of America by
Vicks Lithograph and Printing Corporation

Amsco Publications
New York/London/Paris/Sydney/Copenhagen/Madrid

Compact Disc Track Listing

Contents

1. Pick/Fingers

A Buddy Holly–style riff. Very easy but watch for the off-beat change from ④ to ①.

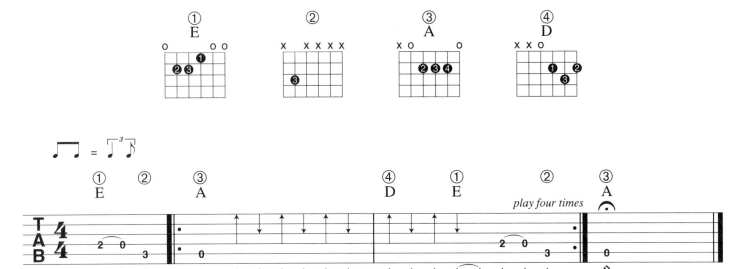

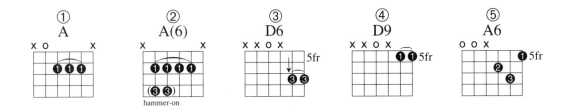

2. Pick/Fingers

This riff has a *soul* sound. Note the slide up to the seventh fret for chord ③.

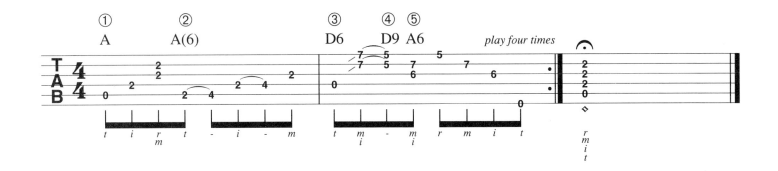

3. Pick/Fingers

The open fifth string under each chord is called a *pedal* note.

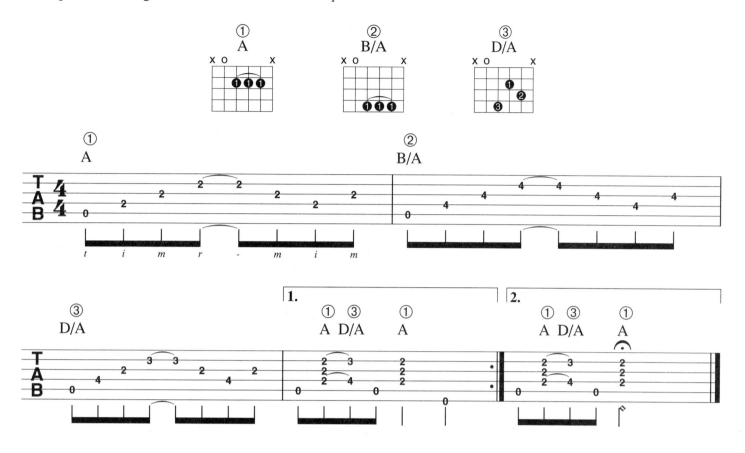

4. Pick/Fingers

Another pedal note through bars 1 and 2. The double pull off from ③ to ④ is typically 'rock 'n' roll'!

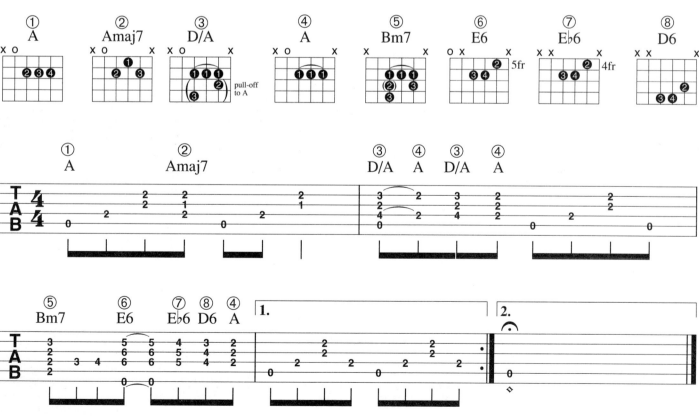

5. Fingers

The best way to get the *slap* sound is to hit the fifth and sixth strings with the bottom side of your right-hand thumb thereby slapping the strings against the frets. Your right hand should be over the sound hole, near the fingerboard to create the best effect.

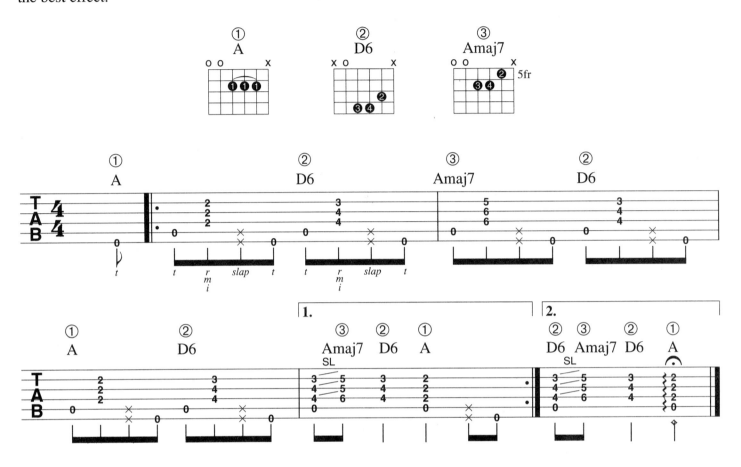

6. Fingers

A popular descending bass line. Try dampening the strings near the saddle with the side of your right hand.

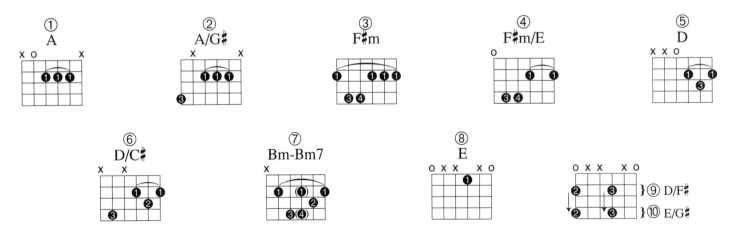

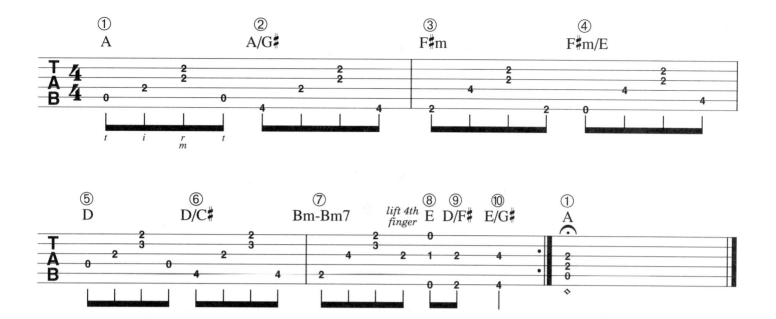

7. Pick/Fingers

This is an A E A progression played in thirds on the second and third strings.

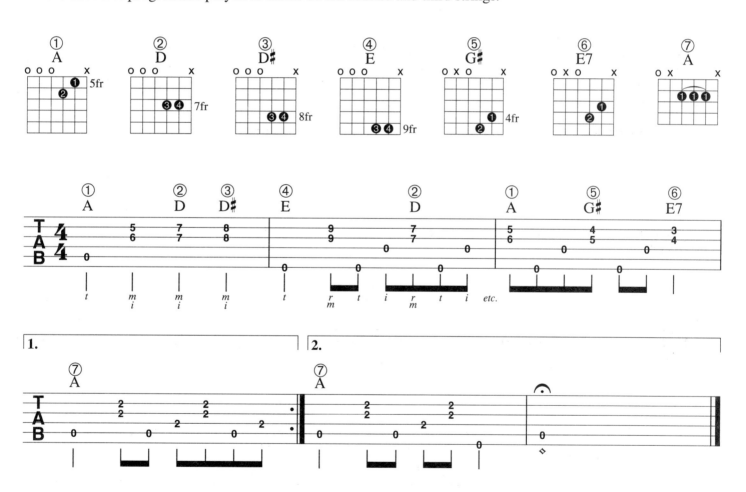

8. Fingers

This riff has a heavy rock feel. Watch out for the left-hand fingering. You can get a snappy sound by pulling the strings with the right hand as you play.

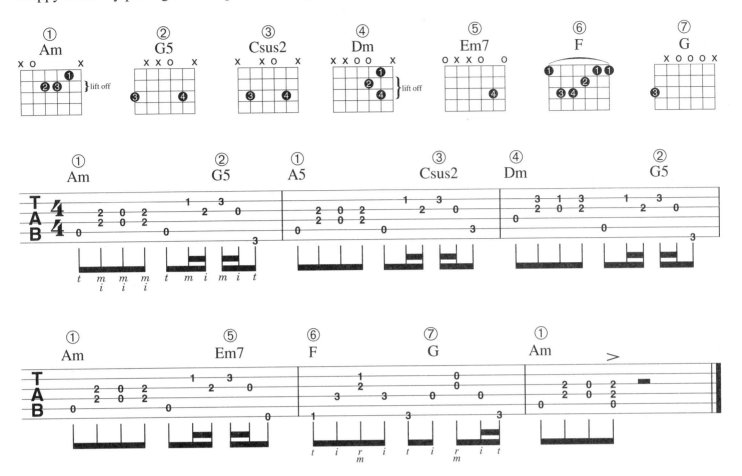

9. Fingers

This is an interesting way to deal with the common Am G F G Am progression.

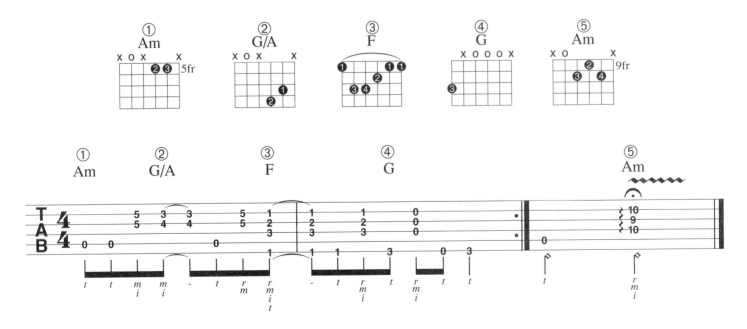

10. Fingers

Stairway to where? This one keeps climbing until ⑤ before descending to ①.

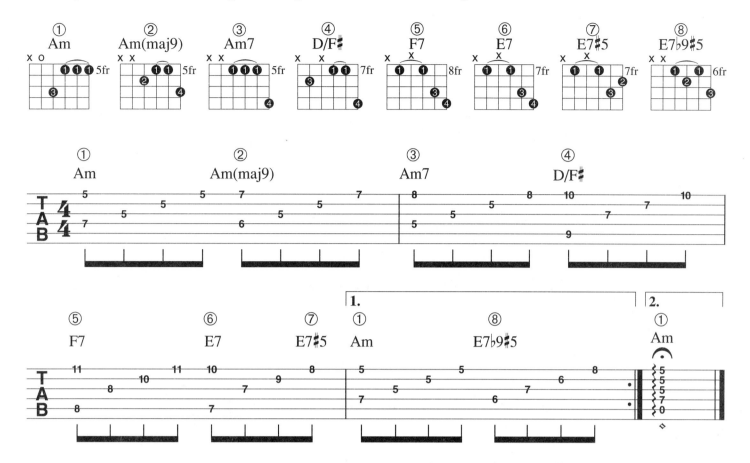

11. Fingers

From *Autumn Leaves* to *Parisienne Walkways*, this has to be one of the most romantic sounding progressions of the century.

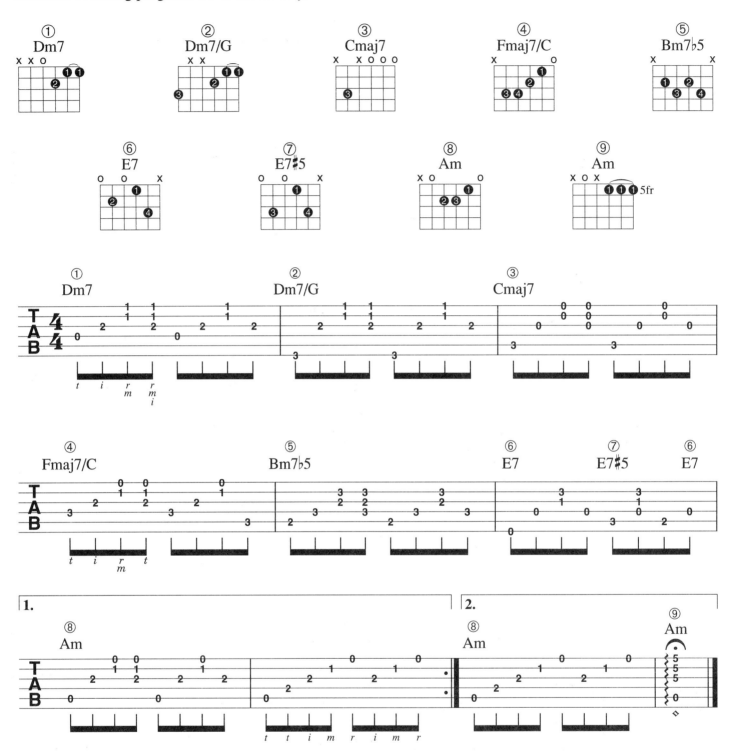

12. Clawhammer

Like the Stray Cats, but this is an old riff. Keep the sixth string dampened and make the most of the glissandos on ⑤.

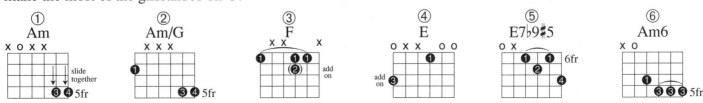

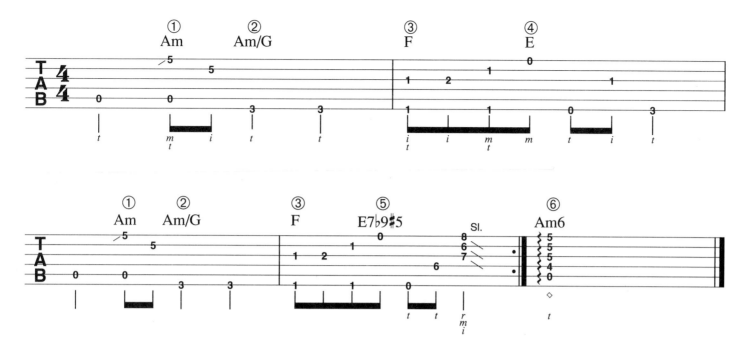

13. Pick/Fingers

This riff has a funky sound. Watch the double hammer-ons. Dampening with the right hand helps to keep the feel.

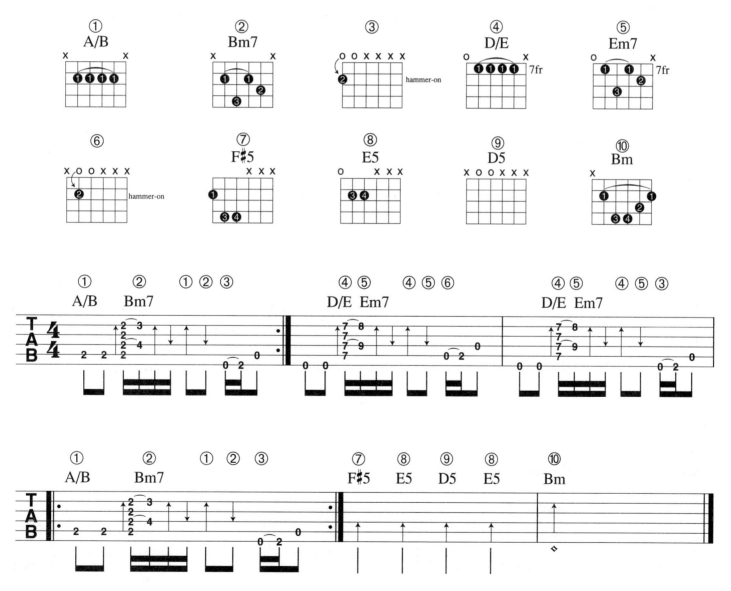

14. Pick/Fingers

It's usually better to avoid big moves up and down the fretboard when changing chord. Here, the correct voicings mean you never have to move more than one fret at a time.

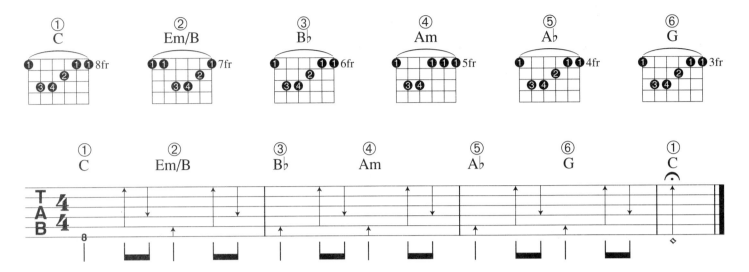

15. Pick/Fingers

There are some great chords in this progression centered around the first fret on the second string.

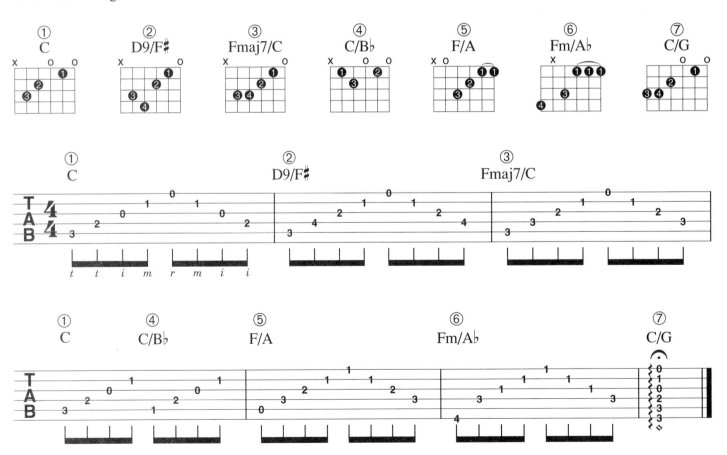

16. Fingers

This has two pedals notes—the fifth and second strings—both C notes. Keep the right-hand thumb going solidly throughout.

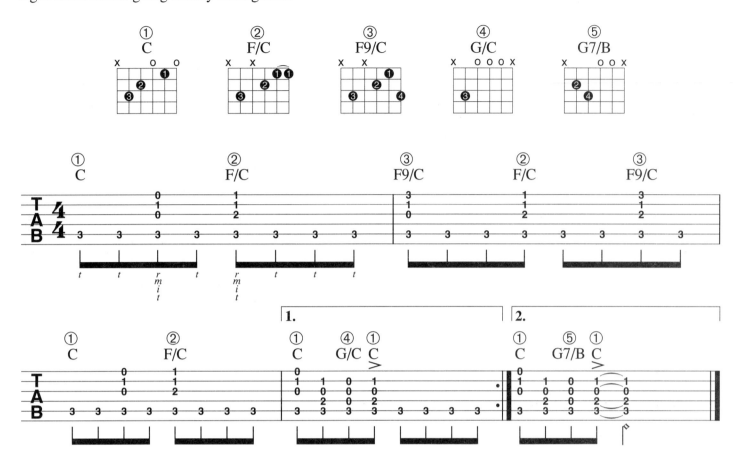

17. Pick/Fingers

This riff uses both augmented and diminished chords. Be careful not to sound any of the strings marked x.

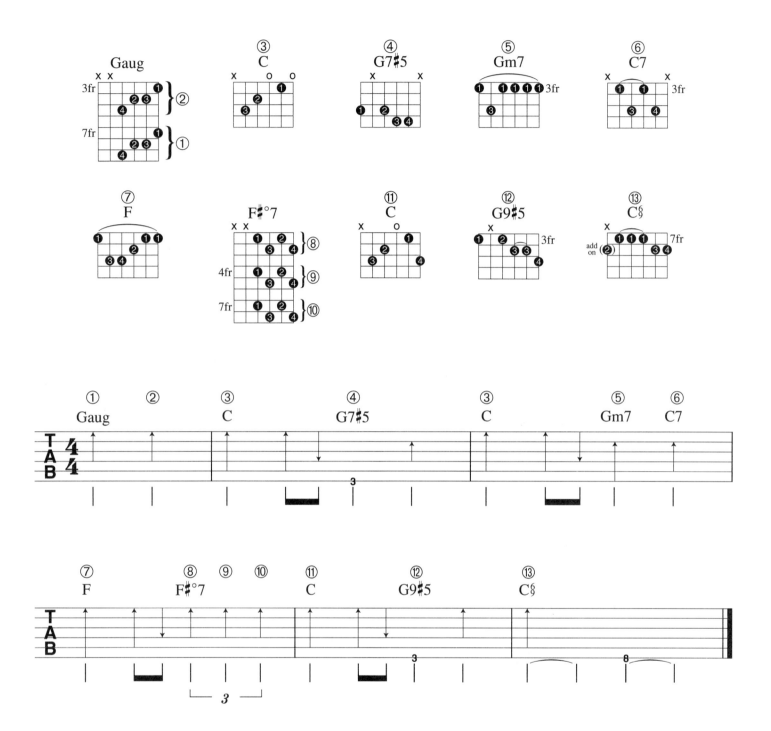

18. Fingers

What's unusual about this funky riff is that the right-hand index finger plays the same strings as the middle finger. Master that *t i r m* pattern and the rest is simple.

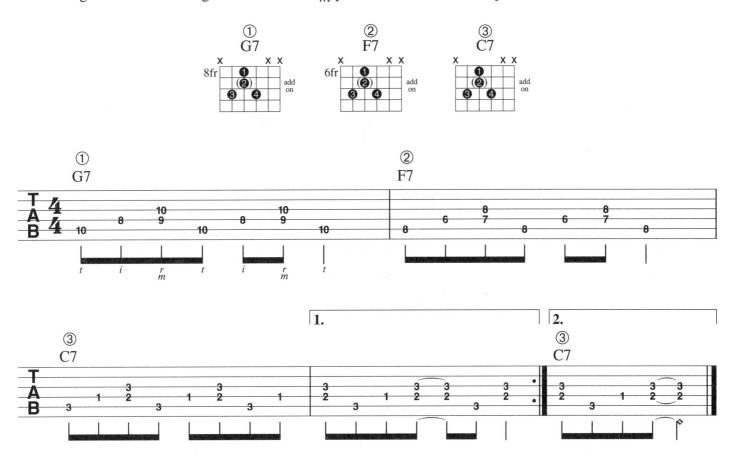

19. Pick/Fingers

This time a D pedal note is used to great effect under a moveable chord shape.

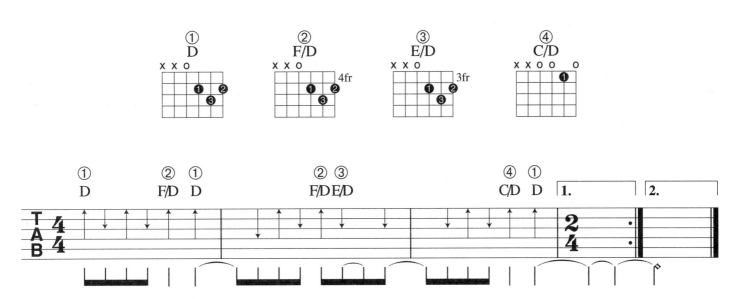

20. Pick/Fingers

Here's a great way of making the sequence D G A sound more interesting.

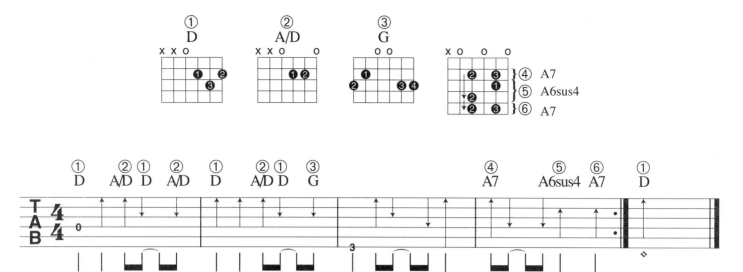

21. Fingers

You need to tune your sixth string down a whole-step to D for this one. The repeated right-hand pattern *t i $\frac{r}{m}$* gives the sequence a syncopated feel.

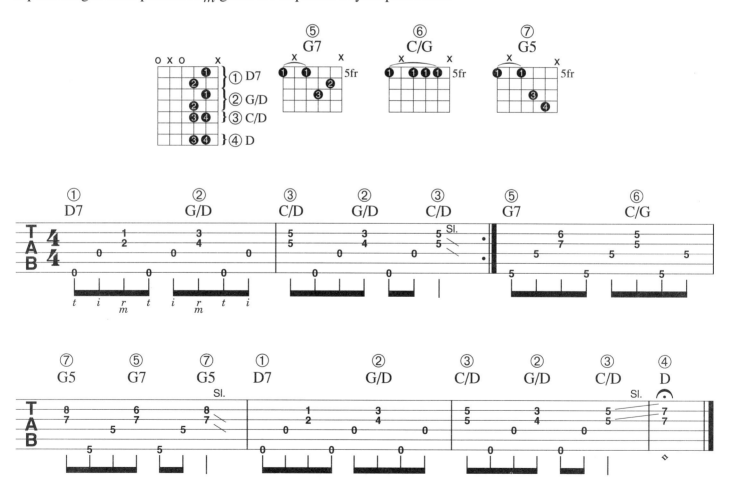

22. Pick/Fingers

A simple sequence that sounds great—just a moving D shape and a fifth string hammer-on.

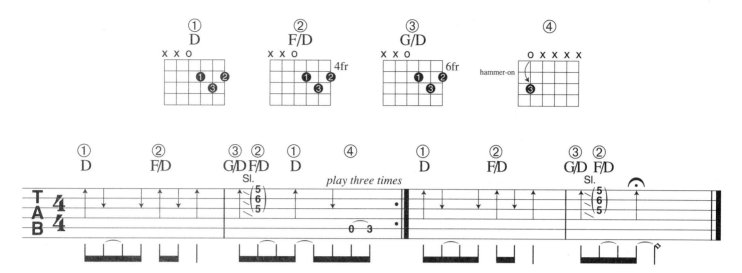

23. Fingers

Another example using the *t i* $\overset{r}{m}$ pattern. Think of the $\overset{r}{m}$ as being like a brass section—adding short crisp jabs to the music.

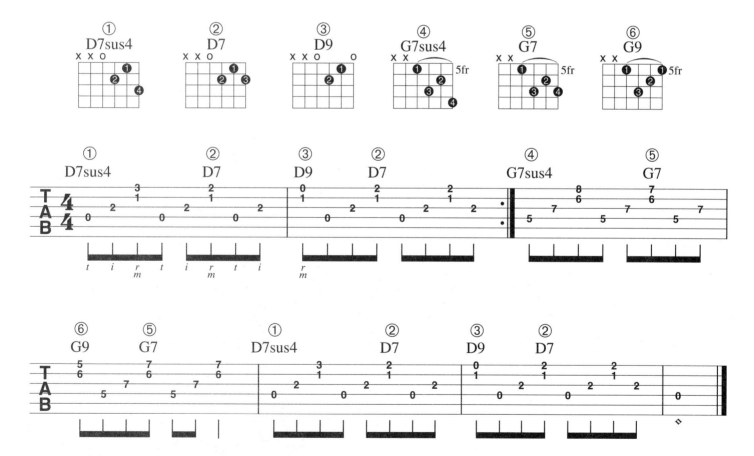

24. Fingers

Dire Straits—or slightly classical! In bars 2 and 3 each melody note is harmonized
by a different chord.

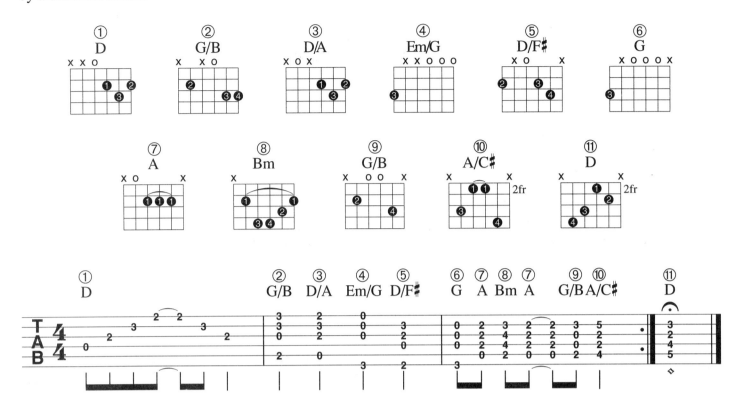

25. Pick/Fingers

A simple descending bass line in Dm. Be careful not to block out the third string
from ⑤ onwards.

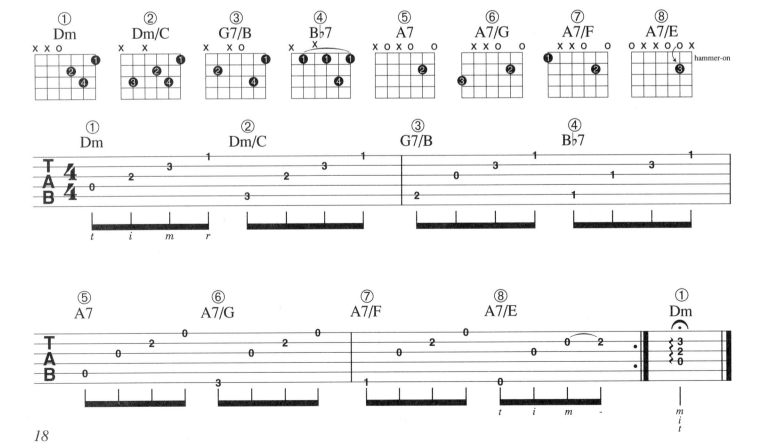

26. Pick/Fingers

This riff uses a pedal D through a Dm Bb C Dm progression.

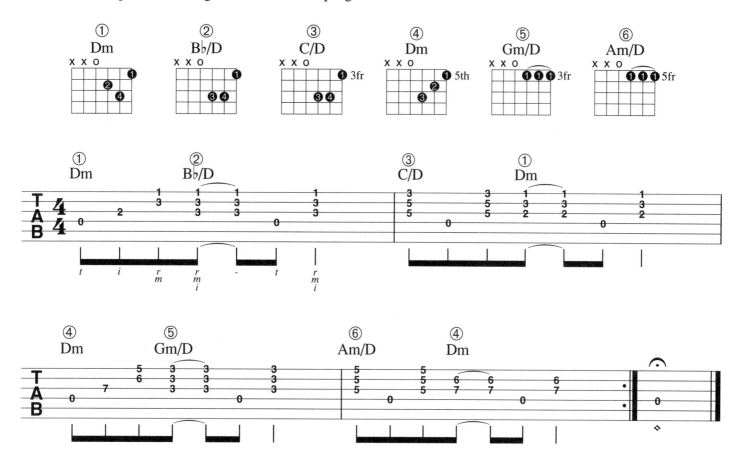

27. Fingers

To get a meaty sound from ③ and ④, try putting your right-hand index finger on the third string to damp it. Then you can really pick hard with your thumb. Don't forget to tune your sixth string down a tone to low D.

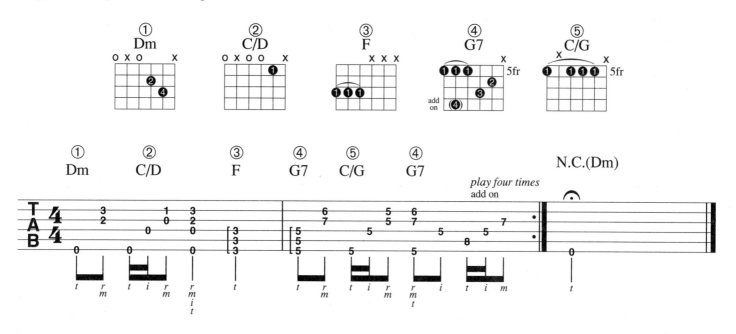

28. Fingers

Getting that Dire Straits sound on solo acoustic guitar means using some awkward shapes, but it's worth it!

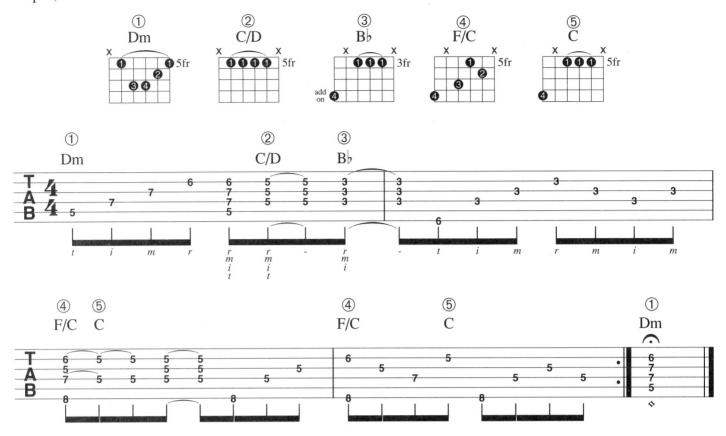

29. Fingers

Nothing difficult here, but put some meat into the ② ③ ② sequence in bar 2! (You need to tune your sixth string down to low D.)

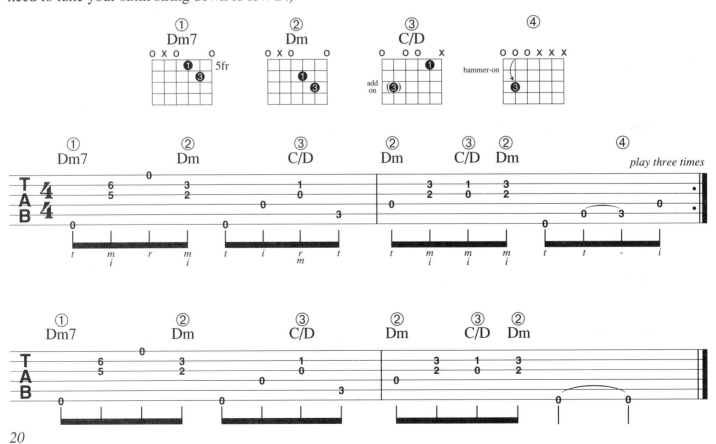

30. Fingers

Keep the sixth string tuned down to low D. This riff has the melody in thirds through bars 1 through 4 and in sixths from bars 5 through 8. Watch the ⑤ and ⑥ change in bar 6.

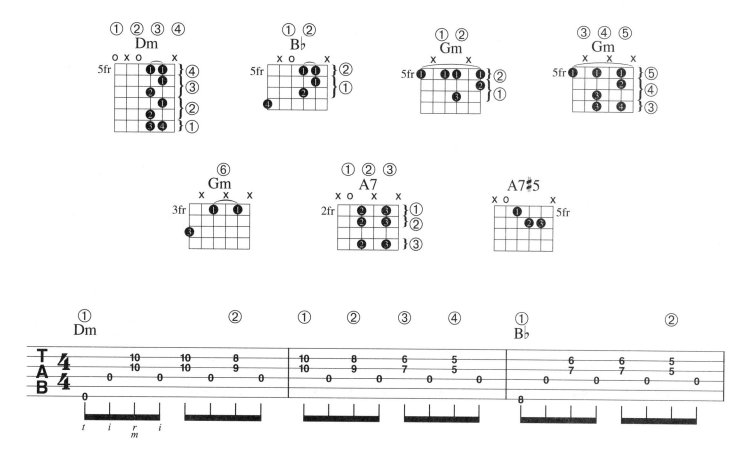

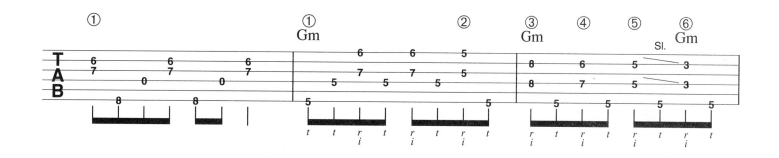

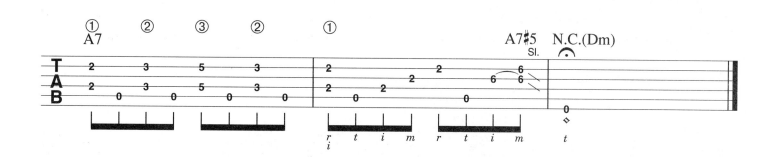

31. Pick/Fingers

A funky Jimi Hendrix style riff. The 7♯9 chord is typical of soul/funk music.
Check out some James Brown tunes.

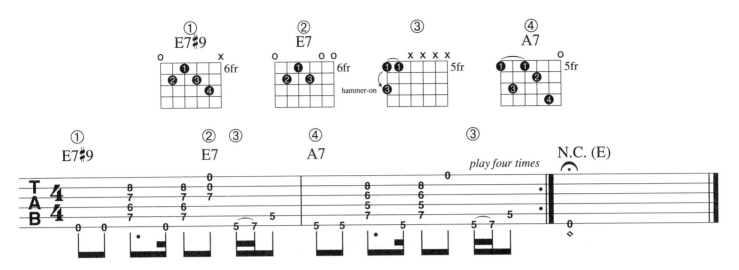

32. Pick

This is a typical rockabilly/country sequence. To get a big sound, strum from the
elbow, keeping the wrist and fingers straight, using a heavy pick.

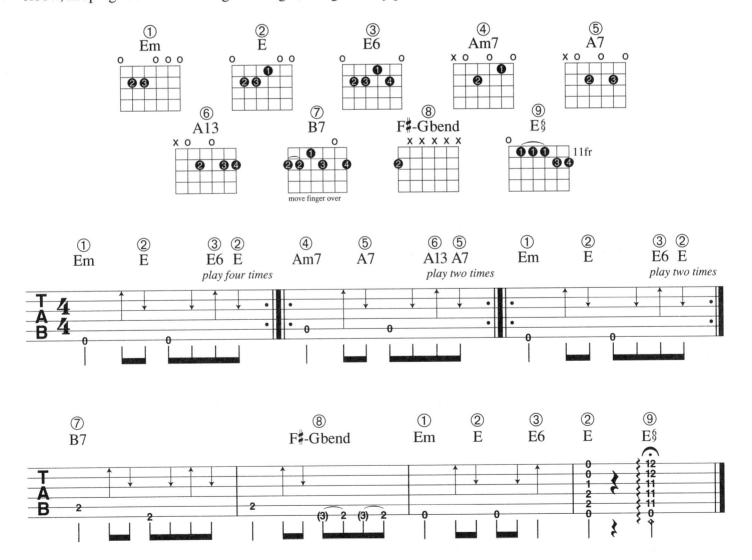

33. Fingers

Slap the fifth and sixth strings with the side of the right-hand thumb to get that percussive groove going!

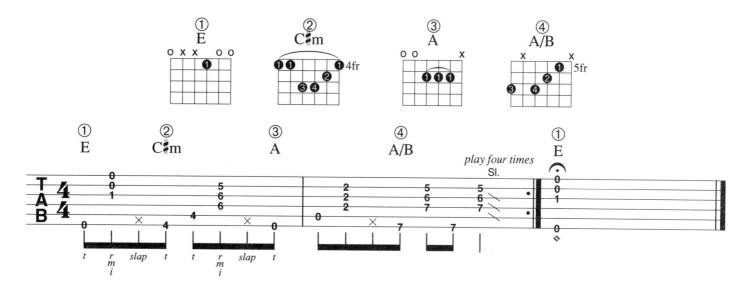

34. Pick/Fingers

This is much easier using fingers. Watch chord ⑤—it's a bit of a crush on the second fret!

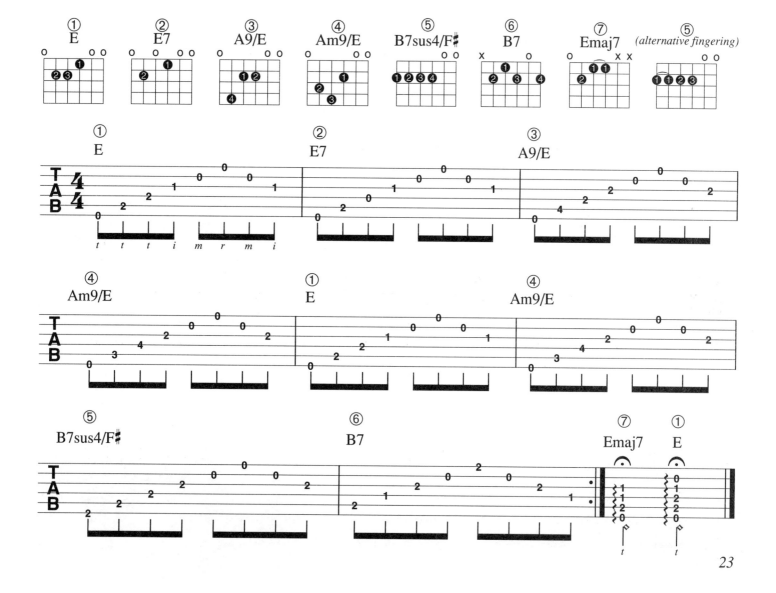

35. Fingers

A really slick riff! Bars 1 through 4 are simple once you've got the right-hand
pattern. Chord ④ can be built up adding each finger in turn.

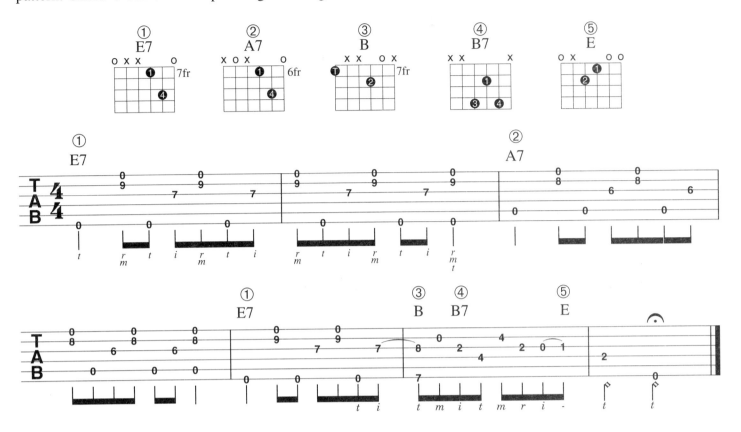

36. Pick/Fingers

This one's much simpler than it looks. Just remember to keep that second, third,
and fourth finger shape held down—only the first finger moves.

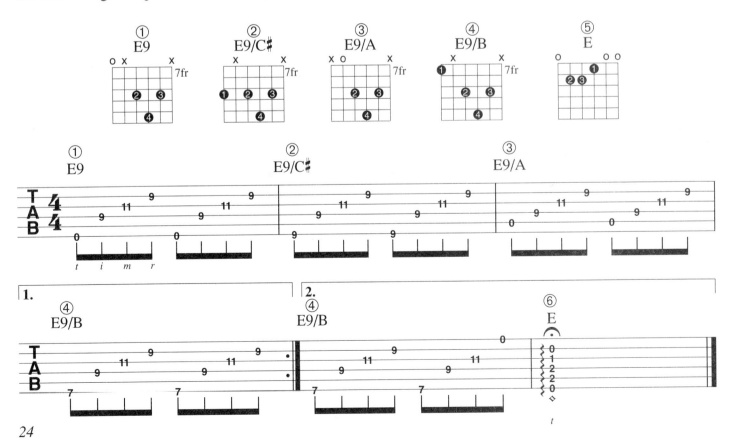

37. Pick/Fingers

Another funky Jimi Hendrix style riff based on a simple E chord.

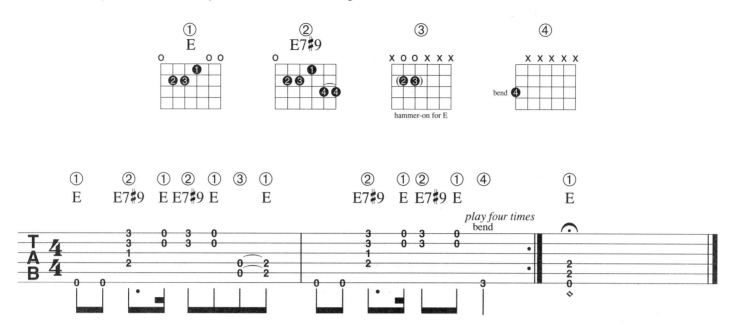

38. Pick/Fingers

A simple three-chord progression, but watch out for the *doubled* rhythm in bar 2.

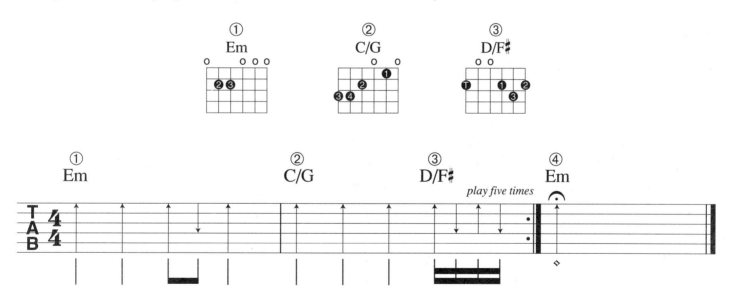

39. Fingers

A simple descending bass line in Em. ① ② and ③ could equally have been placed
on the fourth string, but I prefer the fatter sound of the fifth string.

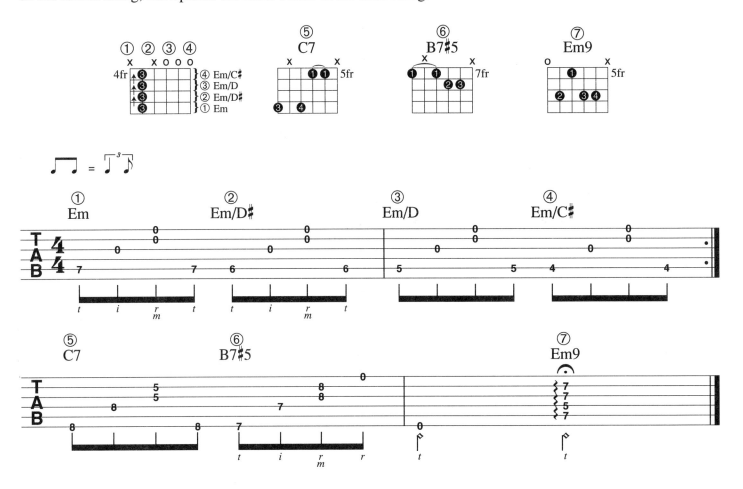

40. Fingers

A simple riff on the common Em C D Em progression. It's the syncopation at ②
and ④ that makes it interesting.

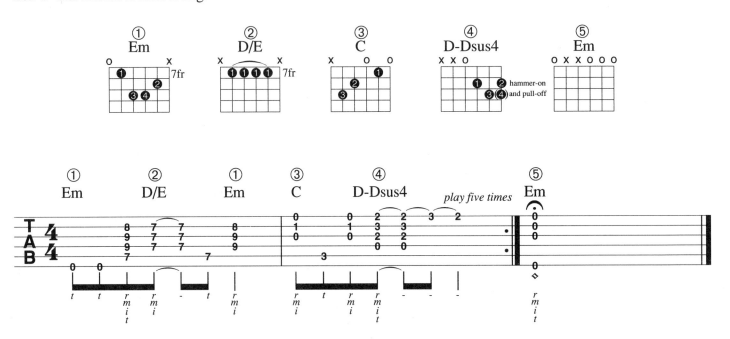

41. Fingers

Another percussive slap riff with a Doors-feel to it.

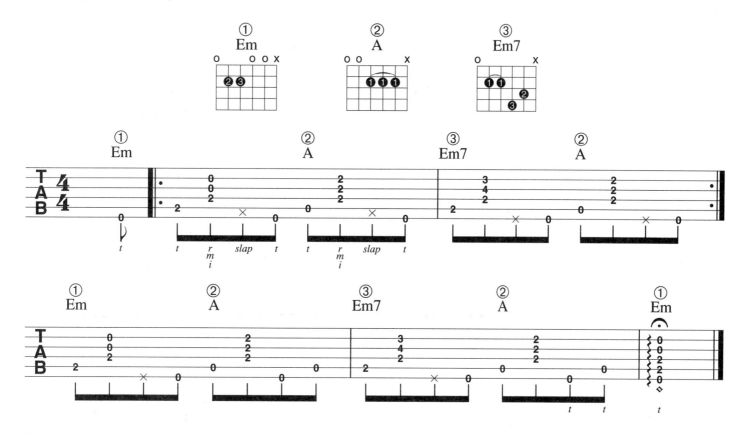

42. Fingers

The ascending line on the fifth string through bars 1 and 2 is very effective. Don't forget that swing rhythm, otherwise the triplet in bar 3 makes no sense.

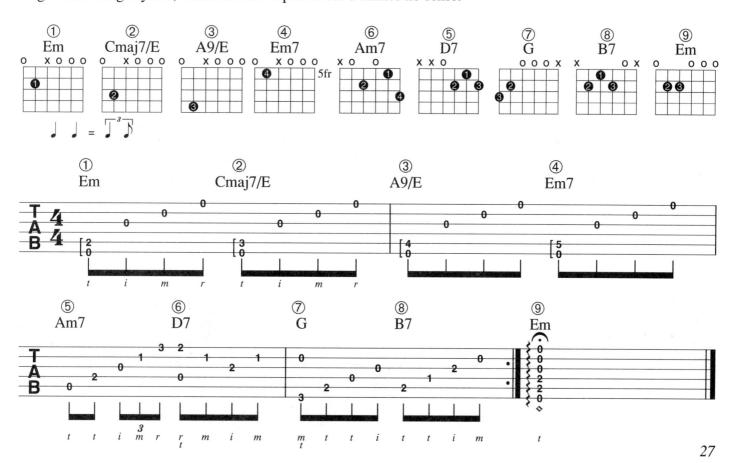

43. Pick/Fingers

To play the glissando (Sl.) at ④, strike the top string then, keeping it pressed down, slide your left-hand index finger all the way back to the nut.

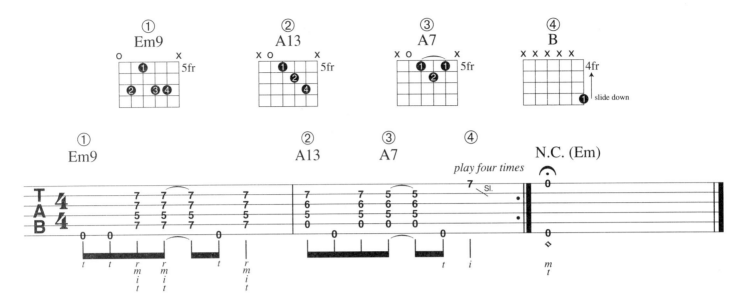

44. Pick/Fingers

Play this one near the bridge to get that bright clean sound.

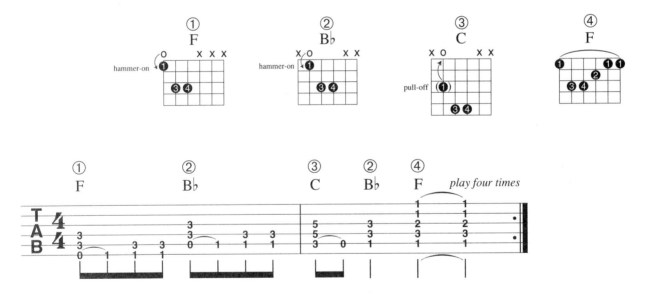

45. Pick/Fingers

Country rock style—dampen the fifth string in ① and ② with the side of your left-hand third finger.

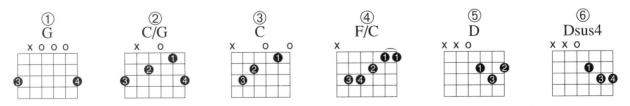

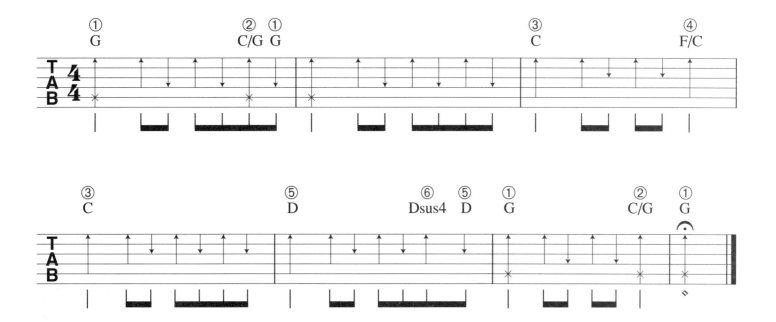

46. Pick/Fingers

Old fashioned rock 'n' roll. After each bend, take the third finger off the string in order to deaden the note.

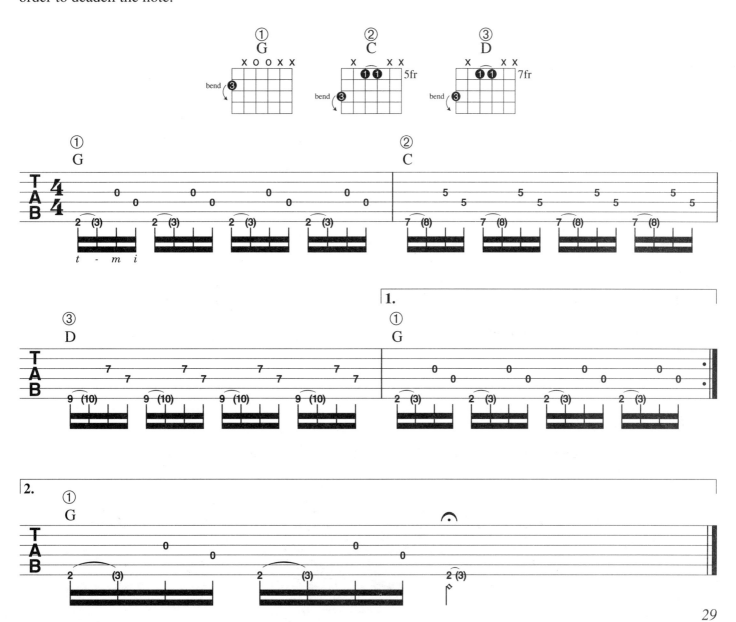

47. Pick/Fingers

A great rhythm and blues riff! For the tap, use the right-hand ring finger to tap on
the pick guard.

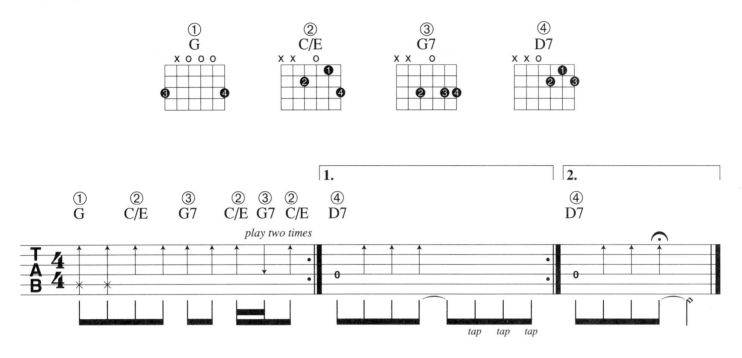

48. Pick/Fingers

This riff uses a pedal G note in the bass throughout. Watch out for the syncopation
in bars 5 and 6.

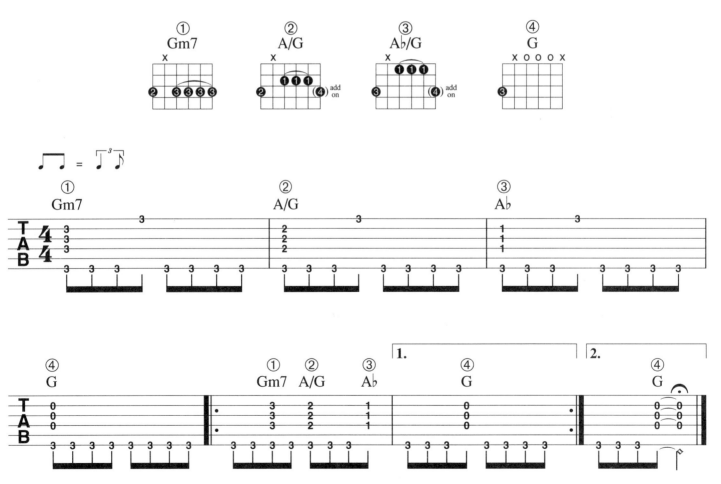

49. Fingers

Play this near the bridge to get that funky sound.

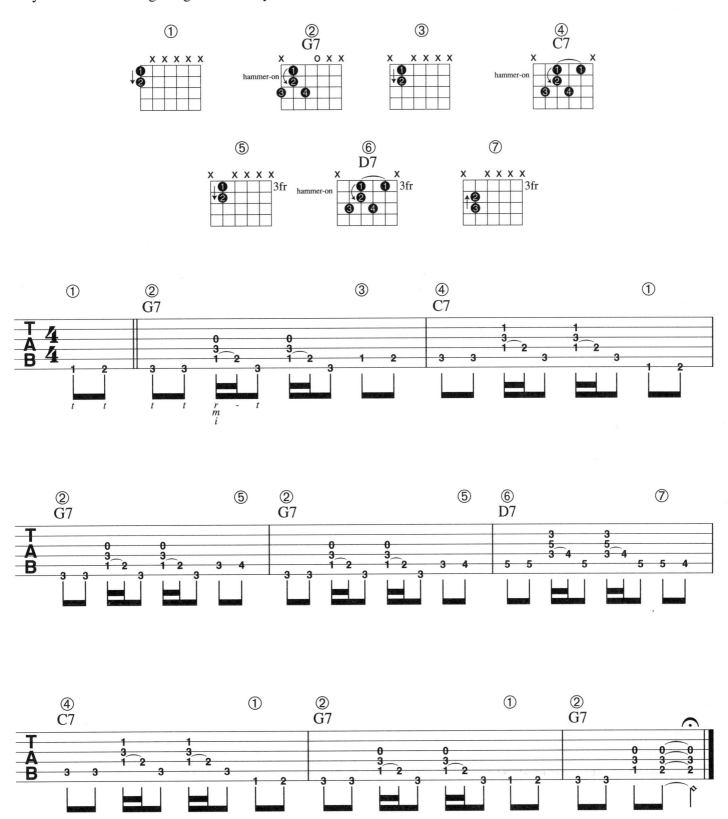

50. Pick/Fingers

Finally a rare outing in G minor. Keep that right-hand pattern rolling smoothly.

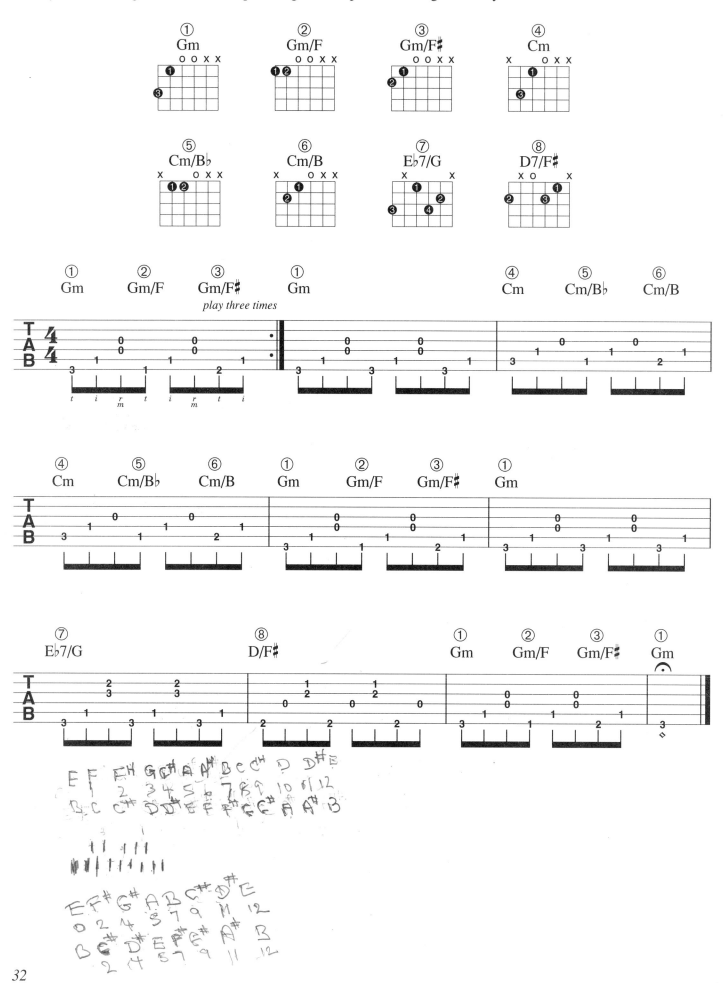